Reema Jafar

Reema Jafar, a fourteen-year-old living in Kuwait, originally from Kannur, Kerala, India. She loves reading books, solving puzzles, writing, and is always curious about the wonders of science. She has been selected as one of the speakers at the United Nations General Assembly Youth Parliament Science Summit 2024. Reema is also a presenter on Kuwait National TV. She began writing poems when she was just nine years old. She participated in the National Children's Science Congress and was selected to present a research paper at the Kerala Science Congress. She also loves playing table tennis and participated in a national-level school table tennis tournament. Reema cherishes her childhood, but she feels that it is going away quite fast. According to her, every parent should plan to create the best childhood for their children instead of only thinking about their children's future. She believes poems are like magical messengers for her thoughts. When she writes poems, she expresses how she sees the world and how things work in her mind. To her, poems aren't just words; they are like a secret code that makes you feel things and think about big ideas. Through her poems, she attempts to make people think and feel with her about the world and life.

English Language
Blooming of Life
(Poems)
by
Reema Jafar

♦

Published in September 2024
by Kairali Books Private Limited
Thalikkavu Road, Kannur.
Ph : 0497-2761200
E-Mail : kairalibooksknr@gmail.com

♦

Cover Design
Aromal O. P.

♦

50/24-25/Sl.No.1617/200/NS.18.6
ISBN 978-93-5973-828-4

Blooming of Life

Reema Jafar

Kairali Books

Reema Jafar's poetic musings show unusual maturity of thought and felicity of expression, considering her age. I have no doubt she has a poetic gene in her and this potential will certainly lead her to greater heights as she passes through the experiences of life, reads more, and polishes and updates her craft through constant meditation, writing, and rewriting. I wish her all the best.

K. Satchidanandan

DEDICATION

To my family

ACKNOWLEDGEMENT

The author deeply appreciates the communication she had with the renowned poet K. Satchidanandan, who generously agreed to review the poems and encouraged her to publish them as a book. He also contributed by writing a few lines about the poems included in this book. Without his encouragement, this book might not have been published. Thank you, Sir.

Special thanks go to Mr. Pradeep Chandroth, who has graciously agreed to write a preface for this book. His insightful feedback helped to improve the content of this book.

The author acknowledges the publisher, without whose backing this book would not have come out the way it is now. Thank you to the Publisher.

The author also expresses heartfelt gratitude to her parents and her sister, Reeya Jafar, for their invaluable support and encouragement that played an important role in the completion of this book.

PREFACE

Wisdom is not a function of age. This is what comes to mind when one goes through Reema's brilliantly crafted words. Reema's realization of everything around her is continuously increasing from strength to strength since she wrote her first words at the very young age of nine. Gratitude towards the abundance that humanity has been blessed with and a keen sense of ownership and accountability towards preserving the same are very evident in these nuggets of wisdom that she is sharing with us. Reema's deceptively simple words are beseeching us to read them again and again. With every reading, one gets a different perspective of the young poet's vision. In Reema's world, everything, living and nonliving, exists for a reason, and this is the very same reason that she is trying to ensure that we are aware of 'Blooming of Life' is indeed the blooming of a young poet, who is set to inspire a whole generation to wake up to the realities staring at us and to get them to contribute to making the universe a better place to live.

Pradeep Chandroth
(Translator of 'The Vaidya')

CONTENTS

You Are You

Although the trees were bare,
Laughter filled the air,
Dodging the snowballs that came her way,
She smiled, happy and gay.

If life were perfect,
More clear and direct,
As that sparkling white snow ball,
Perhaps, it'd be time for her call;
The time of her life
With not a hint of strife.

From her mind she opened a cage,
Letting out wisdom too much for her age;

Life is not perfect,
You are you
And you are as perfect as it gets.

•

Heed to Nature's Call

Nature is bound to call
When we make trees fall;
Nature is bound to cry
When we make life die.

When we pay no heed,
She will take her lead;
For when she grows, we glow;
When she burns, we churn.

It is nothing but love and care,
That strides like a mare;
In the world so tall
When we heed to nature's call.

•

Peace Will Never Cease

His hands covered with blood,
He put on his hood;
It wasn't time to rest
It was time to move to the west;
For there was a fight
That started like a candle light,
Ended up like a raging fire.

This was no time to look at a rose
And reminisce his family,
But to mount his horse
And fight his rivalry.
There shall be an end to everything,
Like the freezing winter turns to spring;
It shall cease,
And come to the ever-longing peace.

•

Blooming Of Life

Opening my eyes, I began to rise;
What is this place, I thought in a daze;
Is this a new race, am I to win;
Will there be hurdles to furnish;
When will I finish.

Time flew by, and where was I;
Still in my race, trying to find my place;

The race of life,

Furnishing my strife, enjoying happy times;
While trying to earn some dimes.

Like every race, my race too will finish;
But unlike every race, everybody has a place;
Life gives everyone a chance to win;
No matter who they are, and how they win.

When your chance blooms,
Don't think about the dooms;
Shine your best,
Before it's time to rest.

•

Your Turn

Soaring in the sky,
The eagle keeps an eye,
Where its prey lay
On a stack of hay.

Down it falls like lightning,
Looking perfectly frightening;
With clenched claws,
Loudly it caws;
Catching its prey
With satisfaction and gay.

Use the chance that comes to you,
And try not to screw;
For, in life,
Only one chance you've got,
Don't let it rot.

•

The Magic Touch

All alone in a deserted place,
With only sand and the sun's rays;
Where nothing grows, but thorns,
A place so forlorn.

Yet, she's perched up high,
Sailing on a ship that strides;
Magic that makes it move,
On a hot summer stove.

It's God's touch,
Even when there's nothing much;
That allows life to grow,
And happiness to glow.

●

The Banyan Tree

I used to be a little seed,
As small as a bead;
One day I began to grow
Knowing I have a long way to go.
I became a little plant,
Then a little tree;
And then, a large banyan tree.

I spread my leaves, far and wide;
With a flock of birds at my side,
A little bird made a nest
To get some rest.

With my wines children played,
Under my shade men laid;
With a little squirrel on my bough;
An army of ants marching in a row.

So many things
Happening around me,
Shows the value of my little seed
As small as a bead.

Precious

Emerald green is life
Sapphire blue is a resource
Amber yellow is a guide
Diamond silver is knowledge
Amethyst gold is character
Ruby red is love

Oh see, the gentle blessings by our side.

•

Time is Merciless

Time ticks away
In a merciless way,
Use it the right way
Or life shall go astray.

Only one chance you've got in life,
Don't fill it with strife;
In life, even if you regret,
Time cannot be reset.

With every second you take,
Your future is at stake;
Mark, your time is yours,
By none can it be taken away;
Except by your misdeeds.

•

Endangered

We are late
To see the planet's weight,
Only when it turns against life,
Will we see the strife
We have brought;
Far worse than a drought.

Do we know what nature means,
When down it leans
Giving enormous landslides,
That gracefully glides,
When it razes houses,
We awaken and rise.

Now we know
We must make a vow
To nature we shall bow.

•

My Country

I am filled with trees, plants and flowers;
I am filled with seas, oceans and rivers;
I am filled with valleys, mountains and deserts;
I am the green country, India.

I am filled with knowledge;
I am filled with wisdom;
I am filled with secrets;
I am the wonder country, India.

I am filled with temples,
I am filled with mosques,
I am filled with churches,
I am the religious country, India.

I celebrate Christmas;
I celebrate Diwali;
I celebrate Eid;
I am the festive country, India.

I am filled with states;
I am filled with people;
I am filled with helping hands;
I am the united country, India.

I am filled with joy;
I am filled with love;
I am filled with happiness;
I am the happy country, India.

●

Happiness We Seek

If I could visit the Sun,
I'd stare in gay
At the Sun's rays;
I'd let my heart sing
At being under the Sun's wing.

If I could visit the Stars,
I'd look down low
Immersed in the Star's glow;
I'd let my eyes see
Happiness and glee.

Need we go this far
For the happiness we seek,
For it's something God has given for free.

•

Road To Paradise

Where the soul lies,
There is a beautiful place called Paradise;
A place where everyone wants to be,
A place where everyone is full of glee.

However beautiful this place may be,
There's only one road you can see;
A path for only two or more,
Go and find the right road;
Out of our reach it never is,
It's the road of kindness and bliss.

•

Dreams Fly High

Up in the sky,
In the cloud so high,
There lies a world
With seas and trees;
With day and night;
With bears and hares;
With beagles and eagles.

The world I talk about
Is the world of clouds;
I wish I could go there,
Which is why
I let my dreams fly high,
To live up in the sky.

●

Teachers

I have learnt many things new,
I have learnt many things from you;
I have learnt many things from this world,
With the help of my teachers.

I have seen many things new,
I have seen many things through you;
I have seen many things from this world,
Through the eyes of my teachers.

I have made many things new,
I have made many things with you;
I have made many things for this world,
With the vision of my teachers.

•

Endless

The last rays of the sun hit the sky,
Like the day's last sigh;
Colors of the rainbow filled the night;
From behind the clouds came the moon shining
bright,

The sky was filled with stars,
And I got a glimpse of mars.

Every day will end,
But you've got faults to mend;
For at the end of every day
Time still ticks away.

•

Rain

I am a little mystery
That falls from the sky;
Like little diamonds on the grass I lie;
I come for a little while
And make the world smile;
Vanish into thin air,
So as to not leave the world bare.

●

Nature's Gift

High up the moon so bright,
With its shining light,
Safely it led the huge ship,
Stopping it from a dangerous slip.

The sun so bright and hot,
The amount of light it offers is a lot,
Helping the huge ship that still sails,
To avoid cries and wails.

It's nature's gift
That helps the world to shift,
Helping mankind to shine.
Giving them what was truly fine.

•

The Way of the World

One little step into an unknown place,
Aware of any dangers she may face;
But escaping was not a choice,
Instead, ready to fight and raise her voice.

Stand up for yourself in life,
If not, others will fill it with strife;
Life is amazingly nice,
Only if you are wise.

•

Role

Everything in this world has a role,
It could be a coal
Or a stone wall;
A small creeping snail
Or a huge swimming whale.

One does not judge by size
If he is wise;
For what matters is wisdom,
Not the size of his kingdom.

●

Barriers To Break

The air went rushing about her,
All she needed was to be a little quicker;
She inhaled the breeze once more,
Every muscle of hers sore;
She flew past one and all;
This had been her call.

Your barrier is yours to break;
It could be a wall or a lake.
Take all you have for the sake,
For it's your future that you make.

•

The Way of Life

Tears streamed in his eyes
As he said his last good byes;
She'd be gone,
But life would move on;
She'd go her way
Yet what had he got to say?

Yet, this is life
No matter what the strife;
People walk on
Leaving you alone;
Go your way
Or life shall go astray.

●

Divinity

The building was chipped,
The paint was ripped;
No one stopped by it any longer,
It was thought to be a goner.

Yet somebody stayed different,
It was just the matter of a few bents;
Determination was what it needed,
And you would have succeeded.

The road to life
Will have some strife;
Dark, eerie places
Is one of it's phases;
But beyond lay sunshine,
The reason life is divine.

•

Choices

She caught the first autumn leaf,
As she heaved a sigh of relief;
Gone was the scorching heat
Autumn was here to greet.

The wind whipped past her,
Causing her to stir;
Life is full of choices,
Whether or not you want to rejoice;
The world is full of sunshine,
Do not bring in the whines.

●

Life's Pendant

With flailing arms she fell,
She had no time to dwell;
Yet the ground she never met,
She was caught instead.

Had she not been caught,
Affected she'd have been a lot;
A small thoughtful act
Could have a lot of impact.

A chain life is,
Not a pendant is to go amiss,
For it may lose it's youthful bliss.

●

A Step Behind Success

Bit by the icy wind,
The air was getting thinned;
A step was all he needed,
And he'd have succeeded.

His limbs refused,
He was beyond bemused;
Success was a step ahead,
It was a step he dread.

Only a chance he got,
Should he let it rot;
He had to move on,
Whether or not he won.

•

Wrecked Humanity

A loud thud was heard,
Nobody said a word;
As silence hung in the air,
To move, they did not dare.

It happened every day,
What were they to say;
There is no gain
When they cause pain.

To savor the massacre of a child
Is not so mild;
The shattering of humanity
Is too much of a calamity.

•

Life's Puzzle

Shading her was a tree,
Beneath it, she was free;
Away from the life sorrows,
Watching the singing swallows.

If life were full of bliss,
She wondered what she'd miss;
It wasn't life nevertheless,
For every life had something less.

We may not have something in life,
Nevertheless, we must survive
'Tis the way God has made it
In order to make every piece of life's puzzle fit.

•

Ready To Race

With a smile on her face,
She steadied herself for the race;
T'was the time she had been waiting for,
She couldn't want anything more.

Life had been rough,
She'd been told to be tough;
Yet change she did not,
Instead, she fought;
Courage was all it took
To pull off the hook.

•

Broken Wings

Far out into the distance,
Looking into the trees so dense,
Something flitted away,
As quick as the sun's ray.

He saw the doe dash,
The hind limb had a gash;
The forest was shaken by a roar,
It was a carnivore.

The life of a doe
Was bit of a woe;
The thought in him flitted,
It wasn't very witted;
Life was made to be the way it is,
'Tis your choice to whether it is grief or bliss.

●

The Unfound Treasure

As she heard the earth tremble,
She felt herself fumble;
Seconds after she dashed,
She heard the building crash.

But who was to blame,
The reason was always the same;
Nature was not to rate,
If we do, we face the fate.

Taking nature under our control,
Is not far from a disastrous fall;
For nature's not a book we bind,
It's a treasure we are yet to find.

●

Blind Eyes

As the wind whipped around,
She heard a familiar sound,
T'was a sound so appealing
Yet she had a sinking feeling.

She knew it took something away,
From each passing day.
They were quite good,
But it's time to pull back the hood.

Like gold, the sun shone,
With it the baby chicks were born;
The grass blew with the breeze,
With it went the quacking geese.

The world is full of splendor,
By none should it get hindered;
Yet we have turned blind eyes
On the glowing blue skies.

It's because of God's boon
That we have the glowing moon;
It's because God provided us a hive
That we cherish this life.

•

The Magic Wand

As she stepped across the street,
She fell prey to the heat;
As she felt herself faint,
Somebody came to her aid.

He'd created a depression in the all-smooth sand,
Our actions are like a magic wand;

They disappear before our eyes
Like the clouds that sail the blue skies;
Nevertheless, a mark is made,
So clear it can never fade.

●

The Hour Glass Of Life

She blinked her eyes open,
Wondering what happened;
The last thing she knew,
She had caught a shining dew.

The world she knew was always a hustle,
Different people with different struggles;
They never found time in life,
To push away the strife.

But life is like an hour glass,
Time flies away fast;
It is the moment we cherish,
Which removes the blemish.

•

Ray of Hope

The rain poured away
Creating a dull day;
Then came a small ray of hope,
Telling them not to mope.

A ray of sunshine can be divine
As it smiled at the world;
A ribbon of colors unfurled,
A shining rainbow was hurled.

It smiled down on life
Brushing away the strife;
Along with every gloom,
A flower will bloom.

•

The Golden Age: Childhood

Her laughter rang into the throng,
She rushed to join the crowd;
Her friends debated on who's wrong,
She was definitely on the clouds.
She had no reason not to be on one,
Her life was great beyond comparison;
She was in her golden age,
Her freedom couldn't be caged.
Enjoy life at the present,

Time does not permit to lament.

●

The Wish of a Lifetime

The star shot away,
Lighting the darkest night of the day;
She closed her eyes and murmured,
And away her wish went like a little bird.

Her eyes glimmered with hope,
At the thought of her wish coming true;
It had been as clear as a sparkling dew,
The blessing of a wish was given to very few.

A wish isn't a blessing,
'Tis a result of laboring;
In this massive world,
You had to do so to be heard.

•

Rampage Of Nature

The waterfall raged like fire,
The water gleamed like sapphire,
Dousing every stone in it's way,
The pebble gleamed under the sun's ray.

The wind made the old oak sway,
Not a single leaf was permitted to stay;
Blades of grass torn apart,
The wind blew as quick as a dart.

Nonetheless, in this stormy creation,
There were few that flitted around in meditation,
Unmoved by the stormy world,
And that was the happiest herd.

•